GET YOUR SATISFACTION

GET YOUR SATISFACTION

A Short Guide to a Happier, More Satisfied Life

ALEX PEYKOFF

www.PublishABestSellingBook.com

Get Your Satisfaction

A Short Guide to a Happier, More Satisfied Life

Alex Peykoff

Published by Game Changer Publishing

ISBN: 978-1-7365491-2-4

www.PublishABestSellingBook.com

DOWNLOAD YOUR FREE GIFTS

Read This First

Just to say thanks for buying and reading my book, I would like to give you a few free bonus gifts, no strings attached!

To Download Now, Visit:

www.GetYourSatisfactionBook.com/Freegift

CONTENTS

Prologue 1

Chapter One - R-E-S-P-E-C-T 7

Chapter Two - You Get Knocked Down, Do You Get Up Again? 15

Chapter Three - Time Is on Your Side – Yes, It Is 25

Chapter Four - The Blame Game Has No Winners 33

Chapter Five - Free Your Mind And The Rest Will Follow 45

Chapter Six - The Triple Threat That Will Bring You Success 53

Chapter Seven - Have An Attitude of Gratitude 65

Chapter Eight - Are You Feeling Lucky, Punk? 69

Chapter Nine - And In The End 73

PROLOGUE

"Life satisfaction is the degree to which a person positively evaluates the overall quality of his/her life as a whole. In other words, how much the person likes the life he/she leads."

~ Ruut Veenhoven

Are you living a Satisfied Life?

Are you living your best reality by being the best version of you – your authentic self?

Are you living your life to have a more powerful and positive impact on the world?

Are you living each day to the fullest while constantly focusing on your goals?

Are you living into the values that will bring you satisfaction and success?

Are you surrounding yourself with people who will encourage your growth and evolution?

Do you have the courage, confidence, and vulnerability to allow love into your life?

Do you have an open heart and mind to new thoughts and ideas?

I can't pinpoint the exact time when I started making decisions to have a satisfied life. In my 20's, I started to embrace my feelings of passion for nature. When I went snorkeling in Hawaii, I recognized that I felt a genuine sense of contentment, peace, and happiness.

I felt complete.

My passion for a satisfied life became even more focused when my daughter was born. I had a passion to be a Dad to the unexpected, amazing gift, Mia, whom God bestowed on me. That was when I truly found what I call my Passion Purpose.

I realized that I had subconsciously sabotaged my satisfaction in favor of other people's ideas of who, what, or how I should be or become. I quit playing the "should" card on myself, and I started to be thankful for everything that put a smile on my face.

I started to live in the moment, to forget about the past or things that haven't happened yet, and all the false labels thrown at me. I embraced who I am. I stopped trying to be someone I'm not. I was surprised to discover that I didn't have to change anything about myself.

I was happy and content.

I just needed to give myself permission to *be*, to follow my dreams, and to stop worrying. I realized I didn't need anything more than what I have now to be satisfied.

For me, a Satisfied Life is one in which you wake up with happiness from head to toe – a happiness that you share with everyone you come into contact with.

About a year ago, I did a handstand pushup on a wall at a local restaurant. I was just having fun and being true to myself. I didn't think much about it, until about four months later I went back to the same restaurant. One of the waiters came up to me and said, "I want to thank you." I had a "hmmm…" moment. He continued, "You made my night when you did that handstand on the wall next to the band that was playing."

As the saying goes, "People may forget what you say. They may forget what you did. But they will never forget how you made them feel."

If you live by the practices in this book, you will glow with positivity and progress -- both personally and professionally -- with sustainability. You will choose to cease worrying about things that are beyond the power of your will. You will find an element of fun in every task. You will stop focusing on the things you left behind and focus on what lies ahead. You will see how important you are to the lives of those you meet and how important you can be to the people you may have never even dreamed of. You will have a confidence that will bring in more opportunities as well.

Set your goals

If living a Satisfied Life is your ultimate goal, you need to have a clear idea of your secondary goals – your agenda.

Get out a piece of paper. Go ahead and get several. You'll be making lots of lists as you go through this book.

Now, write down the top five goals you believe will lead you to a Satisfied Life. If you have more than five, that's okay. Write them all down, and then narrow it to your top five.

Look at your goals and evaluate them. Is your goal really to be a millionaire? Just to have the money and exist in that state? Or is it to have the money to live a certain lifestyle, travel the world, or provide for your family?

Also, make sure that these are *your* goals and not reflective of someone else's desires for you. Often we aspire for what others (parents, friends, etc.) think we should out of a desire for their love and approval, when, in fact, we were meant for something completely different. You'll learn more about finding your passion in Chapter 6.

Take a moment to revise your goals to reflect the real desire behind them. Take another moment to write down the steps you will need to take to reach those goals.

Now, hold on to this list and keep it in mind as you read each of the following chapters.

Enjoy the journey

Success and satisfaction are not accidents. There are steps you can take to move the needle toward what it is that you want while enjoying the journey.

You shouldn't be waiting until you reach your goals to live your Satisfied Life. You should be living it now while you're working to achieve those goals.

It's not what you occasionally do that brings you joy and peace. It is continuous daily action and effort. And while we should plan and work for the future, we aren't promised a tomorrow. Live in the now.

Imagine that what you do today reflects the growth you experience for the rest of your life.

What would you have done differently today if this were true? What will you do differently tomorrow?

A man walks into a book store and asks the clerk if she can tell him where the "self-help" area is?

She replies, "I could, but that would defeat the purpose."

CHAPTER ONE

R-E-S-P-E-C-T

To develop a Satisfied Life, there are vital skills that you will need to learn and practice. We will begin with respect because it is a critical element that can either make or break your relationships. Respect is the foundation of success with yourself & others.

In this chapter, you'll learn:

- The nuances of how respect is created and broken in the smallest of moments.
- How to directly communicate from a place of integrity when respect is lost, no matter the other person's response.
- The telltale signs of behavior that happen when someone else has lost respect for you, and the direct, compassionate way to address this so you can clear the air.
- What personal practices you can use to show respect to your body and mind.

I'll also share with you how the level of respect that we show others is a direct reflection of how we view ourselves. Some of these habits you may already know, but every time we re-learn a concept, we evolve and transform into a more honest version of ourselves.

What do you think of when you hear the word respect? Where did you learn this definition, and how has it played out in your own life thus far?

It can be defined as an admiration of another person based on your perception of their worth in what they do and who they are.

Someone can say they respect their mentor for their work ethic or their romantic partner for their compassion and understanding. Usually, it depends on the parameters of the relationship that determines what it is that you respect in that person.

Let's take this opportunity to do a respect audit for the relationships you currently have in your life. Write a list either on paper or on your phone. What is each person's relationship to you? What is it about each person that you respect? Do you see how the nature and strength of your relationship affect your perception of certain aspects of their worth?

Maybe your significant other thinks ahead and anticipates your needs, making you a thoughtful dinner after you've had a full day of meetings. Maybe your kids never give up and are always trying out new skills while testing boundaries. Perhaps your business partner is unafraid to be direct and honest in their communication, knowing that in the end, integrity prevails and strengthens relationships.

Whatever the behaviors or characteristics within these people are, look at the list and reflect on how it makes you feel.

Admiration and respect are powerful emotions that bond us together as humans. Intertwined with trust, they help us form healthy relationships and live a Satisfied Life.

Respect is also making sure you're seeing someone for who they are and not projecting past relationships onto them. Assume the best. People are more resilient than you think they are.

Now let's look at how you express respect to others and yourself. Look at the list you just made. How do you show respect to the people on that list? If you were to ask those people if you respect them, what would they say?

One way that you show respect for someone is to speak highly of them while in the presence of other people. Loyalty is an excellent indicator of admiration and can immediately reveal your level of respect for them while they are away.

Direct communication with someone is an act of respect not only to them but to yourself. Each time we approach a conversation with honesty and integrity, we grow out of our fear-driven pattern and into new growth territory. It is an act of respect to express your needs upfront and continue communicating as your needs change. No one can read your mind. Use your words and express your thoughts and feelings.

Is direct communication uncomfortable at first? Yes.

Is it an essential part of creating respect in a relationship? Absolutely.

Living a Satisfied Life means facing every person and situation with integrity and an intention to grow. It may not seem like a big deal, but practicing patience and holding back instead of acting impulsively will significantly reduce your stress.

What would happen if you viewed stress as a challenge instead of a threat? What would happen if you didn't respond or react in 5 seconds but instead took a deep breath and choreographed your response as interpretive dance? Okay, maybe you should just do that part in your head. But find a method that works for you to slow your reaction and give yourself time to think before you act in a way that may be disrespectful to others and yourself.

Why am I talking about your stress in a chapter about respect? Because respect is not limited to how you treat others. Respect for yourself is just as important. Stress is harmful to your health. Each time you perpetuate those negative patterns, you are harming yourself – disrespecting yourself.

Another way you can disrespect your health is by eating poorly when you know your body deserves better. Studies show that our mood and behavior are positively influenced by what we choose to eat and drink.

You *don't* need to interact with people who don't align with your values and show you respect. You *do* need to respect yourself.

Have you ever experienced road rage, either as a victim or the one experiencing the anger? Have you ever been challenged on the road? What came up for you? How did it affect you? It's the feeling of being disrespected for many people that makes them feel challenged and triggered in these moments. They feel disrespected, and they become defensive. "How dare they think less of me?"

The example mentioned above is a reflection of my reality. I was head-butted once by someone in a fit of road rage. Yes, I'm serious. It is moments like these when we choose to either respect ourselves and the other person involved or continue to escalate the emotion.

I restrained, counted to 100, took a breath, counted to 100 again, and smiled. Bless his heart. And sure, I might have been thinking that in the more Southern sense of the phrase -- a touch of condescension with a heavy dose of sass. But all of that happened in my head, and then I was able to slow down and take stock of the situation.

Once I was able to see the situation without the filter of my reactive emotion, I was able to see what was going on for me and remember that something must be going on for him as well. I had projected emotions from other things going on in my life onto this altercation with him. As I'm sure he was doing to me as well.

Whenever someone treats you with disrespect, you need to be able to come from a place of growth to be able to look at their hurt without taking it on. If you don't take things like this personally, you can treat them with respect, no matter how they are treating you.

Respect is neither imposed nor begged. It's earned and offered.

Remember: Buying into and feeding into someone else's disrespectful agenda creates a negative situation. This is important to keep in mind in business as well as personally.

It's okay if you haven't been the best at expressing respect and practicing emotional regulation when feeling disrespected. It takes practice and consistency.

To live a Satisfied Life, you must choose to show up with respect for yourself and others around you. You must choose to begin the practice of expressing respect to other people along their journey in life. If you cast shame, blame, or resentment onto someone else instead of respect, you lose every time.

This is not the agenda. The agenda is to be positive, content, and respectful. If you don't follow the agenda, you lose moments to grow. You lose moments to connect. You lose yourself.

If you follow the agenda, you will see positive results in all areas of your life. Restaurants will stay open late just for you if you treat their staff with respect and kindness. You will have deeper conversations if you hold space for and are interested in someone else's thoughts and experiences. A warm smile goes a long way. Professional collaboration will prosper, and your true satisfaction within yourself will expand.

Think of all the times you've treated people with disrespect. Now go back into your memory and watch that internal video of that event but add respect and create a new scene. What did you see? How did it feel? What's the worst that could have happened? Would it have been all that bad? It's one level of growth to see where you made a mistake, but it's quite another to have an apologetic conversation with the person you disrespected.

That doesn't mean you need to become friends with the person you are apologizing to. Just clearing the air may be enough. Be open to an array of responses. Some people will be appreciative, and some won't respond. What matters most is that you owned it so you can move forward.

Respect is a positive experience, and it's *free*. Disrespect is negative and can be very expensive.

In the world we live in today, it has become popular to show disrespect or disregard if someone doesn't match our socioeconomic status. You have no idea what's going on in that person's life, and no right to judge. Who might be judging you in the same way? Break the cycle of negativity. Before you cast judgment on someone you don't see as "equal," look in the mirror & apologize to yourself for introducing that negativity into your thoughts.

It's your life and your choice. What will you choose? What will you *DO*?

CHAPTER TWO

YOU GET KNOCKED DOWN, DO YOU GET UP AGAIN?

When life seems all stacked against you, what you do with it determines your success and satisfaction in life. Your choices can allow you to sleep soundly, or they can keep you lying awake with regret, wishing you could do better.

"It's not how many times you get knocked down. It's about how many times you get back up."

~ Vince Lombardi

The Rocky Balboa films are a prime example of this kind of tenacity. What do you remember the most about him? Of course, it was his triumphs, his wins. Imagine if he hadn't gotten back up?

"Every champion was once a contender who refused to give up."

~ Rocky Balboa

No matter what deck of cards you have been dealt in the past or present, you are in control of how you play the game. You have a choice.

You're either a prisoner of the past or a pioneer of your future. Be a pioneer of your future, and take control.

This world deserves the best from you. You deserve the best from yourself.

You may find yourself feeling hopeless. Even when you feel like you're face down in the mud and people are stomping on your back, put your hands under your shoulders to push yourself back up.

Failure is simply the opportunity to begin again, this time more intelligently and with more experience.

These situations are like working out. The obstacles you face help you discover how strong and capable you are. You won't build muscle or endurance if you don't put in the reps. Just like you'll never be forced to tap into your ability to be resourceful and positive in the face of adversity if you're never tested.

I have been taken to trial in my own life and had to defend what I knew to be true. This did not feel good. What does feel good is knowing I can get through adversity. That it won't kill me, and in fact, it will make me stronger than before.

The trick is to utilize the situation positively to learn about your abilities. Use the opportunity to learn what to do differently next time, but don't dwell on it. Focus on your agenda to achieve a Satisfied Life.

At some point, you need to choose to move forward.

If you feel yourself stepping into the victim role, set a timer for 12 hours, and then redirect your thoughts to something positive and productive. Allow yourself to feel it for the moment, then stand up strong. Invest your energy into making a plan to move forward instead of staying tethered to the past or letting anyone else's negative actions continue to impact you.

Here's what to do when someone is trying to knock you down:

1. Don't take it personally, no matter what it is.

2. Eat well and drink lots of water. You may think ice cream and potato chips will make you feel better, but during stressful times, it's more important than ever to take care of your health. When you neglect your health, you are increasing your stress.

3. Surround yourself with people who cheer you on and help you up when you get knocked down.

4. Pep talk yourself and stand back up! Reinvent yourself a bit if you must, but always *stand back up.*

Your emotional resilience plays a massive part in how you perceive what shows up in front of you and how you move through it.

You're right if you think you can, and you're right if you think you can't. It's ultimately up to you. You decide to choose how you view your internal and external world. It's the very wrestling with the can and cant's, the dos and don'ts, that can be the impetus to your growth.

No one will remember how many times you get knocked down, as long as you keep standing back up.

Some important things to keep in mind when your world seems to be falling apart:

Nothing is permanent. Everything has its seasons. Even your emotions ebb and flow like the tides. If you're feeling triggered by what's going on, take it as an opportunity to refocus yourself and stand back up. The sun will always rise if you keep moving forward. Smile more often, think positively, and access all the beautiful memories in your head.

Life happens for you, not to you. You'll often find people who fall into the "why me?" victim mentality when unfortunate things happen in life. That won't get you anywhere, and if you've been that person, know that you can change. It's just a pattern you've learned, whether from a family member, friend, teacher, or whomever. Negativity is a killer. It will keep you down when you're meant to rise.

So next time something happens, ask, "What can I be learning from this?" Yes, it may be hard to see the good at that moment, but knowing that it's there is the first step. It's a belief that can change your entire life if you allow it.

Your words matter. I've said it before. Don't fall into the trap of victim mentality. Be careful of the language you use to reflect on things that happen. Questions/statements that lead to dangerous territory may sound like these:

~ "Why me?"

~ "Just my luck."

~ "I can't trust anyone."

~ "Everyone is out to get me."

~ "I suck."

~ "I'll never make it."

~ "I don't get it."

When you use language like this, you give up your responsibility – your gift -- to change what's in your control.

You! Your thoughts, words, and perception of the present matter. What's important is the movement forward, not how hurt you are by what happened, and the possibility of not having the person that hurt you in your life. Take a look at your emotions, manage them, and change your actions in response to them.

Phrases that will help you learn from the present experience and lift you up moving forward sound more like these:

- "What can I be learning from this?"
- "I am resilient and can grow from this situation."
- "I am grateful for this experience."
- "I am meant for more and can teach others through what I am learning now."
- "How does this make me feel?"

Can you feel the difference between these statements and the ones in the paragraph before?

People around you might feed into your negativity without even knowing it. It's up to you to keep that in check.

If you haven't noticed, others can – consciously or unconsciously – encourage you to stay small by interjecting phrases like "Oh, I feel so bad for you," "So sorry that's happening," "They're the worst," or "What a jerk."

Remember, just one short chapter ago, when we talked about respect and direct communication? Here's a great place to practice that. Maybe they want to encourage you but don't know how. Try asking them to encourage your growth rather than giving you sympathy.

Don't let people devalue you. *Do* surround yourself with people who know your value- - people who bring you peace versus those who pull you down. Many people may mean well when they say these things, but the words can still be destructive.

Living a Satisfied Life involves surrounding yourself with people who can hold a space for your emotions and then ask you what you're going to be doing differently moving forward. Look around at the people in your life right now. Who has kept you frozen in an unsatisfied life instead of lifting you up? Can you talk to them and explain how they can help you grow instead of holding you back?

The answer to that may depend on whether they have your best interests at heart or their own agendas. These can be people who have not reached their aspirations and may even be subconsciously trying to keep you from reaching yours.

If there is anyone like this in your life right now, distance yourself. When you are moving towards living a fully Satisfied Life, it is essential to have people in your life who are doing the same. This may mean spending less time with certain friends or family members whose ideals don't align with your own.

Friends and family members may have a very specific idea of who you should be, which can be hurtful and limiting to the unique person you are. Your rate of resilience and recovering to your true self will be determined by your inner workings and how you value yourself.

That is why we are addressing both together right now. Even if everything is going well for you today, evaluate your inner thoughts and the people around you. Life can change quickly, and if you keep your foundation of support at an unconditional high level of truth, you will be prepared for a faster recovery rate to your true happiness.

Life doesn't always give you what you think you want, but it will provide you with precisely what you need when you least expect it. Be ready when the door presents itself, and open it with confidence, positivity, and a smile.

Or keep it closed, complain and frown. See what moves you forward or keeps you frozen in fear. And (you know it has to be said here) *let it go*. Go ahead. You know you want to sing it.

Seriously, though. Release the things that are keeping you from opening that door.

Your life is like a book. Not all chapters are going to be great. Some will be better than others, and some will provide the conflict and challenges that make the happily-ever-after that much better. You get to think about how you want to write the next chapter. What do you want it to say? Start here, create, and move forward.

Many successful people have a short memory of failure because they keep moving forward. Failure isn't the end. It's the opportunity to begin more intelligently. Learn from what happened -- don't focus on it. It's an opportunity to change, reevaluate, and choose differently for a better tomorrow.

How do we replace all of the dissatisfied thoughts that can consume our natural purpose to be satisfied?

As a society, we have been falsely programmed to over-tell and relive negative experiences and,_more importantly, under-appreciate the positive things that bring a smile to our faces and others. This counterproductive pattern will prevent you from being content, fosters negativity, damage your mental wellbeing, and ultimately attract the same.

Misery loves company, but happiness elevates yourself and others. This may shock you, but happiness loves company too.

Try this simple experiment. Stand tall, walk down the street, and smile at a stranger. What happened? How did it make you feel?

Now walk down the same street slumping, with an emotionless expression on your face. How did it make you feel? Did you notice how others responded?

Break the cycle of dissatisfaction behavior, one positive thought at a time.

However, you cannot simply tell yourself to stop thinking about negative events in your life. You know you've done it. How'd that work out for you? Yeah, that's what I thought.

Instead, try replacing thoughts of negative memories with happy and satisfying moments in your life. (Your brain is like a hard drive full of millions of videos to choose from).

Don't get mad at yourself for obsessing about dissatisfaction. It will only devalue your happiness. Positive thoughts will lead to a Satisfied Life.

The choice is yours.

CHAPTER THREE

TIME IS ON YOUR SIDE - YES, IT IS

There's a reason the term "time management" is a cliché. It's used so often because it is viewed as a critical component of success. But the concept needs to be reframed. (If you've heard this before, bear with me anyway. Deeper learning comes from seeing new perspectives.)

Successful individuals consistently give the same response in terms of time management. They understand that it is not *time* that needs to be managed. It is energy and prioritization.

To achieve satisfaction and success on a level you have yet to experience, you need to change the way you see things. You need to change your relationship with time. In other words, tackle what is most important first. Don't just focus on what seems to be urgent. Focus on what's essential to achieve your goals.

How often do you have a list of what needs to get done, and somehow you end up checking off all the things that don't move the needle forward? Busy work isn't productive. It's a transactional action instead of a transformational one.

The Rolling Stones were right. Time is on [your] side. (Yes, it is.) Time is not the enemy. Time doesn't change anything unless you do. Time also is not there to be managed.

You're right if you think you can, and you're right if you think you can't. It's ultimately up to you. You decide to choose how you view your internal and external world. It's the very wrestling with the can and cant's, the dos and don'ts, that can be the impetus to your growth. Take a minute and think about that. Look back up at that line and let your thinking realign when it comes to time.

You must manage yourself. You must transform yourself. You must see that the term "time management" takes away your power and responsibility. Your responsibility is choosing for yourself what is most important to accomplish, given the time you have.

Many people use the excuse of not "having time" as the reason for their unhappiness or failure to achieve. Your to-do list probably has a number of items that don't provide you with revenue or joy. Delegate as many of those as possible. This skill requires a level of trust in yourself and other people. But if you can successfully delegate tasks that are neither profitable nor fun, you can focus your time and energy on what is most vital for you to accomplish.

It's easy to blame time instead of practicing proper prioritization and progress. It's a pervasive cultural cycle. It's been fed to you since you were young that somehow blaming external factors will make you feel better about your situation when, in fact, it does the opposite.

Stop giving your power away to time. It is not time's fault that you are not finishing what you've started. Time is just an innocent bystander here.

If you want to live a Satisfied Life, getting done what is most important will bring a sense of relief and fulfillment that you will never get from busy work. You know intuitively what needs to get done, and when you are busy for the sake of being busy, you step further from living a Satisfied Life over and over again.

Don't allow your doubts, fears, and past experiences to cause procrastination and lack of progress.

Sometimes your energy is taken by comparison to other people or comparison to the story you made up when you were little about what you'd be doing with your life by now. Or maybe you're still wondering what you want to be when you grow up. Instead of owning this, you keep spending energy and time on these thoughts. Stop doing that, and start spending the same amount of time on what matters. Your goals!

Use the exercise below to re-prioritize and move forward on what you want in your life. Then identify every way you are giving your power away in those situations. You can only use the time that's given to you, so manage yourself first.

Step 1: *Write out the top 5 things you've wanted to do and have yet to do. The things that have been nagging at you, whether they are future dreams or current things you need to let go of to move out of a lower gear into your high-*

er functioning self. You can write a list longer than 5, to begin with. Just stream-of-consciousness it all out and then narrow it to the top 5.

Examples:

Ending your relationship, moving, making your first $100,000 in your business, leaving your job (or creating a plan to do so), approaching that attractive person, going to the gym (not just signing up), drinking more water, getting a raise at your job, traveling to that place, losing 25 pounds, reading every day, smile more often, etc.

Step 2: *Rearrange your list in order of importance.*

Step 3: *For each of your top 5, write out the top 3 excuses you've been feeding yourself to why you haven't taken action yet. Include time in these so you can see how you've been giving your power away to time instead of managing yourself in the process.*

Examples:

GOAL: To read every day.
EXCUSES: I don't have time. Netflix is more important. I don't like reading.

GOAL: To leave a relationship.
EXCUSES: We've been together for such a long time. I don't want to be alone.
No one else will love me.

GOAL: Lose 25 pounds.

EXCUSES: It will take a lot of time.

I love donuts too much. It's too hard. I've failed every time I've tried before.

Step 4: *Get them done! When your life journey comes to an end, do you want to look back on it knowing you didn't accomplish this list because you blamed time or anything else for your lack of taking action?*

Don't lose this list. There will be a quiz later. Okay, maybe not. But you will be using it for exercises in later chapters.

Living a Satisfied Life means holding yourself accountable and responsible for why you aren't where you want to be while knowing you're exactly where you need to be at this moment in time.

Invest wisely

Time is currency. You've probably heard the term "spending time." I even used it above. Or, "Use your time wisely." Just like money, you should choose how you *invest* your time.

Spending time cheapens the experience while investing time adds value by bringing a level of awareness to the situation.

If you say you are *spending time* watching obsessive amounts of Netflix, you are telling your subconscious that it's okay. "So many other people do it, plus the couch is soooo comfy...."

When you say you're *investing* time watching Netflix, you compel your mind to look at where else you could be investing your time instead. Would it be better to read that book on your nightstand? Would that move the needle towards your goal of increasing your skillset to get the raise you want, or create higher-level conversations in your daily life?

Make sure you're investing your time into tasks and experiences that will get you closer to where it is you want to be.

Fact: When you choose to invest your time in this book instead of Netflix, you are acting like you've already achieved that raise.

Fact: When you sign up with the trainer and (not just the gym!), and then you *show up*, you are acting like you've already lost that 25 pounds!

When you invest your time wisely, you are already that person you want to be, not the person in the past who quit in the past. Now, you're moving forward and investing time in things that will get you to become the person you're meant to be.

The most important thing is to take care of is yourself and your mind. If you haven't gotten that point yet, say it out loud right now.

Now, one more time.

And just for grins (and because a habit is formed by doing a thing three times), say it again.

No, you cannot *manage* time, but you sure can use it as a teacher. How you choose to invest your time reflects your beliefs, excuses, or mindset.

The most successful people often have their time scheduled out to 15-minute marks. They schedule in time for learning, fitness, family, etc. If you're new to this idea of prioritizing, the most important thing is to set yourself up for success.

Set a time block -- an hour, for example. Turn your phone to airplane mode and do the first thing on your list. Do not pass Go. Do not collect $200. Do not wander on websites or social media. Focus. (You'll learn more about focus in an upcoming chapter. For, now, practice.)

You will start seeing time as a tool for developing yourself -- transforming into who you need to be to achieve your goals.

Time is your friend. It's on your side if you prioritize it well. It is not gifted to us to blame and accuse for why we aren't doing what we want to be doing. Time is the innocent victim here.

Whenever you hear yourself -- either out loud or in your mind -- blaming time, catch it. Pivot and start again with a new positive thought and hold yourself accountable. It will endlessly benefit you in taking responsibility and examining what you need to do and what you have been avoiding instead of projecting it outward.

If you want to live a different level of life, you're going to need to change your patterns. If you change your patterns relating to time investment, I promise you'll notice improvement.

What will you do differently now that you see time in this way?

Goal: A Satisfied Life. Now get rid of those excuses and get it done!

CHAPTER FOUR

THE BLAME GAME HAS NO WINNERS

TRIGGER WARNING: This chapter may cause sensations of discomfort for persons who are committed to living the same small life they've been living. Reader Discretion is advised.

Now that you've learned to respect yourself and others, get back up when you get knocked down, and stop looking at time like it's your enemy. Let's identify the one thing that's keeping you stuck.

And of course, how to change it to live a Satisfied Life.

What is it? I thought you'd never ask.

Some may call it "giving your power away." I call it blaming anyone or anything else for you not taking action in your own life.

Culturally we are accustomed to complaining and blaming. This comes from how we are raised and who we surround ourselves with, and how much easier it is to blame external factors than take accountability and responsibility to change our lives.

I'm not telling you to roll over and accept everything or every situation. There is a difference between seeking to right a wrong and complaining/blaming. Returning a broken item to a store isn't complaining. Protesting for a cause isn't complaining. Learn to tell the difference between taking action to right a wrong and merely complaining.

Easier is not necessarily better, especially when it comes to taking responsibility for your actions or inactions. What's worth happiness is worth working for.

It's going to take what I call C.P.R. No, not the practice used on people who are in cardiac arrest. However, it will save your life – your Satisfied Life.

C.P.R. = Consistency, Patience, and Respect

Consistency, patience, and respect are vital while practicing and mastering this new way of being.

You need to be consistent. Build a habit of evaluating your part in every consequence.

You need to have patience with yourself and others. As much as you try to be consistent with this new outlook on responsibility, you're going to have moments where you slide back into old patterns. Accept that you have done it, re-evaluate the situation, and move on.

And you need to have respect for the future you want to have by making this change. The coping mechanism (complaining and blaming) has served you until now, but only to a point. It will not get you to where you won't want to be. Or who you deserve to be.

Blamers don't work well with others, and they tend to have a lower level of performance and a lower level of fulfillment in life overall.

If you have a habit of complaining and blaming in your life, take notice of it now to change the pattern moving forward.

I went to Jamba Juice not long ago, and I watched a woman return her order to the counter. She said, "I ordered two small smoothies, and you gave me two mediums. If I had wanted mediums, I would have ordered mediums."

They had not charged her for mediums, yet oddly enough, she complained. All they did was use a larger cup for the extra leftover. It happens all the time, and most customers are usually happy with it—more bang for your buck, or in this case, more Jamba.

Complaining is a reaction that's ingrained within some people. Make sure you're not one of them.

Think about this for a moment and reflect on your day up until this point. What have you complained about? How important did it seem at that time? Looking back, does it seem less important now? Did complaining make it change? Did it make you feel better?

How about what you've witnessed others complain about? Looking at it from outside the situation, did it seem like a thing worth complaining about? Did complaining change the situation for that person?

Hint: If it's not doing any good to complain about it, then it's not worth complaining about. Learn to tell the difference between speaking up about something wrong and voicing your unhappiness just to hear yourself speak.

Complaining is a prerequisite and gateway to blaming. They usually seem to go hand in hand. So if you practice one, the chances are that the other is alive and well.

Don't invest your time in complaining

Remember, way back in Chapter 3, where you learned to re-think your concept of "time management?" Imagine your day (your time) as a pie. You have the same amount of pie as everyone else because, as you've learned, time is the constant. You determine what percentage of your time pie you spend and where you spend it. You can indulge in blaming and complaining, but that wastes your time and gives away the energy needed to create positive change in your life.

Or, you can do this, catch yourself and utilize that same amount of pie for joy- creating activities. (Like making pie.)

Think of the most prominent players in the world right now. Do you think that they surround themselves with people who complain?

Please. Ain't nobody got time for that.

Imagine your goals and desires. If you want to live like one of those players, you're going to need to upgrade your support system.

Take notice of the people in your life who complain, even yourself. Why waste time complaining when you could be transforming?

Remember way, *way* back in Chapter 2, where you learned how it's imperative to get up when you get knocked down? This works the same way. Learning to take ownership of your thoughts and actions now will serve you tremendously when things don't go as you envisioned—practice, practice, practice.

It's like muscle memory. If you tend to complain now when things are going well, can you imagine how much worse you'll react when things go poorly? You'll have a much slower "stand up" rate if you're stuck in complain mode. Break this cycle now. Start appreciating what brings you joy.

You may fail, but you aren't a failure until you start blaming someone else

When you fail (or think you've failed) at something, what do you tend to do?

Imagine back in school. If you got a low score or bad grade, did you own up and say, "I definitely could have studied more?" Or were you quick to find other reasons – other places to lay the blame?

Maybe you blamed the teacher. "They don't like me," "They made the questions too hard," or, "They didn't teach it right." Maybe you blamed your parents for not making you study as you should have. Perhaps you blamed your neighbor's dog for barking all night and keeping you awake.

Parents sometimes get in on the blame game in a situation like that, especially those who view a score or a grade as a reflection of their child's worth. In an attempt to protect their child, they go to the teacher and demand an explanation. By doing so, even well-meaning parents join in on what I call the "Circle of Blame Game" and become an enabler, instead of addressing the only person in control of the effort made, their child.

The pattern of blame often starts at such a young age. It can even begin before the school years. Anyone with siblings close in age has either falsely blamed a sibling for something they did -- "It wasn't me! Sissy broke it!" -- or has likewise been falsely accused.

Diverting responsibility away from yourself in fear of being caught, punished, or embarrassed is a learned behavior with long-reaching consequences. It creates a cycle of identifying your worth by your successes and perceived failures. Those consequences can be catastrophic to your success as an adult if you let them.

It can be incredibly uncomfortable to own your shortcomings -- to acknowledge the fact that yes, you did consciously choose to go out last night instead of staying in and reading or listening to that podcast that could have prepared you for tomorrow's meeting.

Do you hear what I'm saying? Say it to yourself... *I am accountable for my actions.*

It's like blaming your neighbor for bringing over Krispy Cream donuts or even blaming the donuts themselves. (Come on, you know you've done it.) When in fact, you chose to say yes to eating these donuts because you were people-pleasing your neighbor and didn't want them to feel bad. (Or maybe just because you wanted to eat the donuts.)

Now you feel bad because your actions did not stay in line with your commitment to eating better this week. And it's just so much easier not to take responsibility for that choice, once again affirming a habit of blaming external factors for your level of something only you could control.

Especially when it comes to lifestyle changes, blame is the first thing that will take you off course and farther away from your desired result of transforming to your *true self.*

Be careful not to slip into a victim-blaming mentality when there is a circumstance that truly is out of your control.

You don't have to (and you shouldn't) take responsibility for the things you can't control. Instead, acknowledge the thing or circumstance that you can't control and focus on what you can control -- your actions and responses.

To continue moving forward on your desired path, I want to help rid you of your complaining and blaming mindset.

Remember that list of goals you made in Chapter 3? Aren't you glad you kept it? Take a look at your goals and the common complaints and blame games played that are getting in the way of you achieving them.

Example:

Goal: Losing weight.
Blame: Biology and family genes. The belief that you cannot lose weight, don't have time, have failed before, so you cannot succeed, or cannot afford healthy food.

Any of those blaming statements completely takes away your ability to make a positive change in your life. If everyone in your family is physically unhealthy, it does not mean you have to be. Yes, you may have been taught one way of eating, but you can learn a new way. When you were a child, it was out of your control. Now that you are an adult, you control your choices and actions.

You decide your outcome based on your actions. Stop blaming your way out of the Satisfied Life you deserve.

Example:

Goal: Starting a new business.
Blame: No one I know personally has done it. I've failed before and will again. The market isn't ready. I don't know how to do it.

Blaming the market or anyone else is a cop-out. It takes part of your precious pie away from creating what it is you want! And today, with an infinite amount of resources available at your fingertips through Google, social media, and YouTube, it's not a valid excuse to say you don't know how to do something. Leaving it at that will never get you to where you want to go. What it will do is keep you suppressed and unsatisfied.

Keep playing the Circle of Blame Game and ask yourself how's that working out for you. Or, invest some of your time in learning the skills you need, finding and creating solutions, and just working for what you want.

It goes against the status quo to take responsibility and not blame others. Don't fear the things you need to face. To live a life that most people never will, you need to be open and willing to do what most of them won't do in every area of your life.

How do you see blame play out in your workplace?

When a project doesn't succeed, do the people on your team point fingers at each other, or does everyone take responsibility for their contribution to the outcome?

This is what high performers do. They examine the outcome and look at their own contributions and performance to learn what can be improved in the future.

Sometimes people avoid taking responsibility because if they had a part in a negative outcome, it makes them feel wrong and less-than. Often this pattern was learned in childhood. Now is your opportunity to unlearn those bad habits, retrain, and transform to your true self.

The flip side of no longer engaging in complaining or blaming is learning how not to take on blame when it's thrown on you by other people. It's also learning the difference between taking responsibility and blaming yourself.

Nothing in this chapter should lead you to take responsibility for your part of the pie and turn it into a blame and shame game with yourself. This is meant to be an empowering new practice, not a time to continue beating up on yourself.

Living a Satisfied life is not to blame yourself or others. Instead, it is to take responsibility for what you can do differently and then *do it.*

Blame from other people, especially those we love or tend to seek approval from, like family members, can be incredibly heavy. (I really didn't break that glass!)

They say that feeling bad about something shows that you care. This is not necessarily true. You can take responsibility for your actions and recognize that someone else's response to those actions is their choice.

Holding onto blame and anger takes a significant major toll on both physical and mental health. Even longer, chronic ailments such as migraines, anxiety, and depression can come from converting energy into blame instead of responsibility and change.

Stop blaming traffic for you being late or in a crabby mood.

Stop blaming the person who hurt you for your ongoing suffering when you're choosing not to heal (or seek help healing) from the experience.

Stop blaming your upbringing for your lack of fulfillment or success.

Stop blaming the government, your community, small-minded people, your family members, your friends, your pets, your house, your car, your health, your weight, your food, your workplace, your boss, your coworkers, and most importantly, **yourself** for anything ever again.

To live a Satisfied Life, start to get real with yourself. If you've been blaming someone for something, apologize to them and yourself, and then move on. If you've been blaming yourself instead of just owning what you need to change, do look in the mirror to apologize and start *moving on.*

You are in complete control of how you act, think, and move forward from this moment onward. If you find yourself complaining, ask yourself if you can change it to a positive. If there's no solution, then drop the complaint. Why waste time and energy on something you can't do anything about?

Move forward into a new way of being the best version of yourself you can be.

CHAPTER FIVE

FREE YOUR MIND AND THE REST WILL FOLLOW

Most people aren't open to other people's opinions or ways of being. Instead, they tend to view other people as wrong or judgmental. If you have this view in your personal and professional life, it will ultimately hold you back from transforming into a truer and more authentic version of yourself.

Improvement and transformation are about being open -- open to new ideas, new expertise, and new ways of thinking and being.

If you aren't open to the new, then you're content with the old has overwhelmed you. As with many of the practices in this book, being open takes awareness and the willingness to transform old patterns into new, productive ones.

"When I was ten, I thought my parents knew everything. When I became twenty, I was convinced they knew nothing. Then, at thirty, I realized I was right when I was ten."

~ Author unknown

When you're young, you think you know everything. So much so that you are unwilling to listen to anyone else.

You could receive advice from the most respected expert in their field, but if you have a know -it- all attitude, their sage wisdom will most likely go in one ear and out the other. Even worse is when someone is sharing their knowledge with you, and you're so wrapped up in proving your own knowledge and intelligence that your thoughts are drowning out what they have to share.

Behavior like this leaves you less connected and missing out on perspective and information that could potentially change your life.

Where does this start? Often in our youth.

Children create this kind of pattern at a young age when they don't want to listen to their parents or people of authority. Unless you acknowledge and address this, it can be holding you back from the growth you say you desire.

Every person that crosses your path or knocks on your door has something to teach you. It's up to you to extract those lessons and utilize them to your advantage of growth and evolution.

Or not.

Beyond learning it in childhood, why do people stay in this pattern?

Often it stems from a lack of trust in other people. Maybe you acted on someone's advice, and it went wrong for you. Or maybe you're not sure that the person giving you advice has your best interests at heart. Or perhaps they don't know enough about you or your situation.

Sometimes it can come from having someone give you "advice" that is actually criticism in disguise. Even if you just perceived it to be critical, it can still be hurtful. This can feel like a violation of your intuition and understanding of what you want and how you want to get it.

This can often happen in relationships.

I dated a Venezuelan woman for eight years who always gave me advice. At the time, I viewed it as being negative and judgmental. Even though that wasn't her intent, that's what I heard because -- at the time -- it was what I thought she was saying.

I wasn't open to her message because I couldn't get past my perception that she was criticizing me. This limited my ability to see any value in what she was saying because of my defensive reaction.

If you ever take someone's words personally, know that they are most likely triggering a defensive reaction in you. It's your responsibility to see it differently -- to be open and learn.

In the example above, she was expressing her observation that my culture as a whole has little to no passion, especially compared to hers. Now I understand what and how she was trying to convey to me, and I recognize that it was my own perception that was preventing me from hearing it.

This is the case for most people. What we hear may not actually be what the person is trying to convey. Your perception is based on your own experience. Once you understand this fact, it can open a lot of doors and make sense of miscommunications that happen every day between partners.

Be open to the possibility that someone is not judging you personally but just expressing their observations. Once you do this, you will open the door to improvement and unconditional acceptance.

It's harder to take feedback in areas that could be a high trigger area for us. In romance (as I just shared), in business, or when it comes to our bodies and health.

Have you ever had someone share a piece of information with you on how to possibly operate more effectively with your workout or food regimen and completely written it off? I have.

For years physical trainers told me to eat as much protein as I could. Over and over again, as if the protein was the be-all-end-all. Then I finally met a trainer with a health science degree who broke through with his perspective that yes, protein is essential, but so are other key vitamins in my diet, as well as sleep, eliminating stress, etc. If I had been more open to the ideas of others, I would have taken the time to research the importance of protein. I might have even sought the advice of an expert earlier.

Just like in your food, you need a well-rounded mindset and the ability to be open and try new things if you want to be the best you can be.

I know it's not easy. I can attest to this requiring ongoing practice because I have not always been the best at it. Since I've been on both sides of that line, I can see more clearly the benefits of what it is like to be open. I know how imperative this practice is if you want to succeed.

Imagine you're starting a new business or wanting to excel at your job, and you need to do things you've never done before and set out to do it alone.

We, as individuals, don't have all the answers. Unless you are the absolute, unequaled expert on a subject, there will always be someone who knows more than you. And even if you are that expert, someone else will have a different perspective that might lead to a new way of thinking if you open your mind.

When someone gives you advice, they aren't criticizing or judging you.

It doesn't mean that you are wrong, just that there might be a better or new way to do it that you didn't think of or notice.

Coaching has become a hot career path for a reason. A good coach can show you the mistakes to avoid and how to increase your efficiency and overall experience in business. They can do this because they've been there before. Just because they share what they know does not mean they are asking you to go in a completely different direction from your goals.

Expert advice isn't meant to change your goals or agenda, but it can help you adjust the steps you take to reach them. Never change your agenda or goal, just the steps to get there. To do this, you must be open to changing and stepping out of your comfort zone.

How much longer do you think you'd take to get to your end destination if you were not open to getting guidance and advice that would improve your trajectory and speed of arrival?

Imagine you're driving to a meeting in an unfamiliar new city. There will be weather disturbances, but you're not open to the feedback and information provided to you by your maps or GPS. Will you get to your destination or veer off unnecessarily? Most likely, the second one. Odds are, you're going to be late for your meeting.

This closed-mindedness way of being will also contribute to unnecessary stress, confusion, weight gain, anger, miscommunication, poor relationships, loneliness, isolation, health issues, missing income opportunities, and overall low level of life satisfaction.

No one can change overnight. However, you can take baby steps every single day.

One way to go about listening without giving in to an automatic defensive reaction is to listen without responding. Don't nod, or agree, or even make a little "mm-hm" noise as someone is speaking. Stay silent and just listen. Then before speaking, see what comes up for you.

Are you angry or automatically shutting down their perspective? Well, don't do that. Stay open.

When you find yourself being closed-minded to advice, remember how frustrating it is to be on the other side of that equation. Maybe you've also noticed that when someone reaches out to you for help or advice, they aren't open to the answer you give. Sometimes, this is attention-seeking behavior, and you may be guilty of this practice. Sometimes, it's not a matter of whether to listen to advice, but which advice to give more credence to.

When a friend of mine wanted to get into Real Estate, I connected her with an expert in that area to mentor and advise her on how to succeed.

Unfortunately, my friend's business partner was not so open-minded. Like the angel on one shoulder and the devil on the other, my friend had conflicting opinions coming at her from both sides. She'd get advice from the expert, and then her business partner would tell her why she shouldn't take that advice.

She let her business partner's voice stop her from taking action. Instead of objectively evaluating the sources of information, she let fear and doubt undermine the expertise she was being gifted.

Often the best thing you can do when going after a new goal or venture is to clear out those who "don't get it" and stay in your forward-thinking lane by taking advice from mentors and individuals who support you.

Don't waste time with someone who is not as open as you wish to be, or you will significantly reduce your chance of having a Satisfied Life. *Do* stay open to others.

There's a theory that you take on the characteristics of the five people you spend the most time with. Think about that. Write their names down and decide if that's who you want to be like.

Don't be so influenced by people in your inner circle who don't support you unconditionally. If that's where you are, then get real with yourself and make some changes.

You'll thank me later. More importantly, you'll thank yourself.

You have to accept that you might not know everything.

But are you willing to learn?

Improve yourself every day, evaluate yourself every day. If you want to grow, you have to be open to other ideas aside from yours.

Success and satisfaction take innovation in thoughts, actions, and perspectives. It takes putting aside your ego and taking on new ways of being that can help you improve every single day.

If you're not open to other people's ideas, you'll self-sabotage.

Don't create an echo-chamber inside your head.

Do Stay Open.

CHAPTER SIX

THE TRIPLE THREAT THAT WILL BRING YOU SUCCESS

PASSION is the foundation of a Satisfied Life.

*Passion is an emotion to **FOCUS** on.*

*Passion is the fuel for your **HUNGER***

The three values explored in this chapter are those three that I've found to be incredibly important along the path of satisfaction. They are ones to cultivate and "live into" every single day.

If you do, they will propel you forward beyond your wildest dreams. And most definitely past the fears, doubts, concerns, and limited ways of being that so much of our world is living in today.

Passion

If you look up the definition of passion, you'll find a description along the lines of "a strong and barely controllable emotion." It is the nearly uncontrollable aspect of passion that sometimes elicits fear within people. At times, we can be a joyless society, so much so that our nervous systems may find it easy to interpret as dangerous. This can result in people altogether rejecting the experience of passion because of subconscious fear. Instead, they choose to settle and continue to complain about how unhappy they are.

Desire more for yourself.

Passion is a powerful word. Almost as powerful as you are when you embody it daily.

Do you know what you are passionate about?

For me, it's nature. For you, it may be a cause that touches your heart and for which you raise thousands of dollars. It can be about building your career and propelling your business forward. It might be transforming your body and mind into a peak state of being. It could be traveling the world and exploring different cultures.

Time to make another list. Write down a list of things that have brought you feelings of passion and joy. Take notice of how these activities make you feel – physically and emotionally -- when you experience them. This will make it easier to identify what it means to live a Satisfied Life.

What if you don't know what you're passionate about? That's okay. You've already got the paper out. You know the drill.

1. Pull out your phone and scroll through your browsing history on social media, news apps, or even on a browser. Ignoring politics and breaking news, what was the subject matter of the last five posts you *actually* read or watched?

2. If you had a three-day weekend and unlimited money, what would you do? Don't think about it! Just write down the first thing that comes to your mind. Now, I'm sure as soon as you wrote that down, you thought of at least three other things. Great! Write those down, too. There's no wrong answer here and no limits on your dreams and passions.

3. Now, do step 2 again, assuming you had a month off of work and unlimited money. Go!

4. Okay, one more time. This time think big. What if you had a year to do nothing except what you wanted? What would you do?

5. Now take a minute and look at everything you just wrote. Do you see any patterns? Does anything send a spark of joy and excitement through you when you consider it?

If so, maybe you're on track to finding one of your passions. If not, that's okay. Consider this an opportunity to try things that give you at least a little joy and see if that happiness grows. Or, maybe trying one of those things will lead you down a different path that leads to your ultimate satisfaction. Don't be afraid to explore the possibilities.

Whatever your area of passion is, you'll find that it is something you enjoy more than the average person. You aren't here to be average anyway. So, when you find that, you're on the right track.

Passion isn't what society tells you to be passionate about. It's what warms *your* heart and lights *you* up. Only you can decide what you're passionate about.

It may feel uncomfortable at first because identifying and seeking passion- producing activities is a heart-centered pursuit. It takes tuning into your heart and tuning out what other people think is cool or what they *want* for you. Perhaps those people are more focused on what they want for themselves but aren't brave enough to create it in their own lives. So, they may try and tear you down instead, saying things like your passions are crazy, excessive, or unnecessary.

Whatever it is they say, always pivot towards your passions. You exist for a reason and purpose. If you keep prioritizing other people's thoughts over the desires within your heart, you'll continue to wander unsatisfied and frozen in fear. I'm passionate about nature, and I've become more so as I've traveled. When I am consciously working towards feeding my passion for travel and nature, I feel whole and alive. A feeling of inner peace comes over me.

If you start feeding your passions, you'll understand what I'm talking about. It's something I hope for everyone reading this to experience. I want you to feel that sense of completion, total euphoria, and even numbness from head to toes. These feelings are similar to how I felt the day my daughter was born.

In those moments, time appears to stop and continue simultaneously. Some identify the feeling of being in-flow.

Part of passion is trusting yourself and not overthinking. When I'm in-flow and passionate, I wholly embody the present moment. This allows ideas to come and helps me piece things together that an otherwise heightened state of stress would block.

It's the feeling of simultaneously going someplace while remaining utterly still.

When I am enjoying nature and traveling to new places, I sometimes find myself consumed by an out-of-body, blissful happiness, and pure calm. Once you discover what you're passionate about, you can line up your goals to feed these moments.

Focus

Once you've identified your areas of passion, next is focus. Stick with me here. I know passion sounded a lot more fun, but focus is critical to pursuing your passion.

Focus may sound boring because it means saying "no" to impulses and instant gratification. I'm not only talking about the impulse and gratification of buying material things like jewelry, cars, or shoes. Even a relationship may be something that takes your focus from where it should be.

The important thing here is to find your meaning in the word "focus." To see how it brings you closer to the lifestyle you desire, not further from it.

When others spend money on material items that bring them surface-level joy or validation, you can align your thoughts and actions with your passion and focus beyond the temptation.

What are your temptations? (You know what's coming. Do I even have to say it?) Get that paper out and write them down. Take an honest look at your life and list the things you spend unnecessary money and time on.

You've written down the activities that produce passion and joy – the "do these things" list. This one is your "stop doing that" list to clear out the crap that is robbing you of your focus potential.

The instant gratification society that we live in tells us that we "need" things that aren't true necessities. There is also a high percentage of people who don't sit down and do the work you're doing right now. They don't know what they value in life.

If you have a goal and want to achieve it, clear away the things and people holding you back. Set yourself up for success and satisfaction and become a step- forward human being.

This means that focus needs to be a joy-producing activity for you. It means surrounding yourself with people who also operate in this way. Even if that means walking alone for a bit until you find people who fit this standard, it's a necessary part of the process. I support you in that decision, and the kinds of people you want to keep in your life will support you, too.

You will always have tasks to complete that don't, by their nature, bring you joy -- doing your taxes, for example. But you can make it a more joyful experience by creating an environment of enjoyment and focusing on the activity instead of dreading and putting it off. To get excited about doing this task, you can make sure you have good music, a nice view, water, and snacks, and set your phone on airplane mode for no distractions.

There is always a solution. You just need to be open to it.

It's been said that focus is more important than intelligence. Many successful people talk about how their laser focus was a huge factor in their accomplishments.

Focus on what you're trying to accomplish. Then accomplish it. Practice and master this skill, and it will serve you over and over again.

When God unexpectedly brought my daughter into the world, I knew I had to be focused on her unconditionally. I was heart-focused and steadfast, knowing that I was entirely responsible for a new little human being I call Mia.

I knew I had to get educated and gather all the knowledge I could to focus on the task at hand -- raising my daughter. So, I did. Instead of allowing my friends to persuade me to go out and party, I chose to stay in and focus on the most important goal I would ever have. Instead of getting overwhelmed, I rose above the noise and overcame with a level of confidence that I found in educating myself on how I could best execute this new way of life.

You can do this too.

You can be the smartest person on the planet, but without focus, you'll wake up one day wondering how you became unhappy, unhealthy, and completely unsatisfied.

What is one thing you can stop doing today to promote focus in your life?

What is one thing you can do today to promote focus in your life?

Passion, Focus & Hunger are needed to achieve anything.

Hunger

Now that you've seen the benefit of focus, it's time to discover why you're hungry for your goals and why you want what you want in the first place.

Maybe you are hungry and driven because of societal pressures. Or perhaps someone told you in the past that you couldn't accomplish something, so you're on a quest to prove them wrong.

If your hunger comes from a place like that, move past it. If your desire to succeed is driven by that external focus and proving the naysayers wrong, it won't bring you as much satisfaction as an internal driving factor will.

Look back at the goals you wrote down. Where did they come from? Do they come from a place of internal desire for success and satisfaction? Or do they come from external influences? If they aren't truly *your* goals, but goals that have been imposed on you, re-evaluate them.

Acknowledge that the externally driven hunger has brought you this far -- which is great. But then look deeper. Who can you help by creating success and satisfaction in your life? Could it be your child, as it was for me when my daughter was born? Maybe your partner would benefit from your overall happier state of being in pursuit of a Satisfied Life? Or possibly, an increased level of overall health would help for your potential future family.

Be in the present and look to the future.

Hunger will help you stay focused and passionate. Hunger and drive will help you position yourself for success and move past impulse decisions. When you want something with every fiber of your being, you let go of past hurt, pain, and resentment because that will just get in the way.

When my dad was a kid, he shined shoes for a living. His hunger was driven at the time by literal hunger -- the need to have food on the table. It would get down to 10 degrees outside in the winter in Buffalo, but he kept going. Basic needs can drive you, and accomplishing them allow you to be content and satisfied.

It's often easy to identify individuals who do not have these key factors in their day-to-day routines.

Not too long ago, I was in the Midwest, where I encountered a woman. She was ordering Monster energy drinks, gum, and a specific pack of cigarettes. She was clearly in survival mode, not success mode or future thinking mode. Each purchase was taking her away from financial and emotional freedom. She was tied to addictions and the consumer- numbing devices that are always readily available. These things are traps that only hold us back. They aren't going to help you achieve your Satisfied Life.

If you simplify your needs to survive, you can focus on your goals and create some type of permanency. If you can live on $10/day, do it. Then focus from there. Planning for your needs is possible and incredibly helpful while staying focused.

It's your choice to tap into your passions, cultivate focus, and stay hungry. Or not.

People who take few chances often do so because they have placed subconscious limitations on their potential. The next time you are presented with an opportunity, don't ask yourself what could go wrong. Instead, think about what could go right. Don't worry about how you'll do it. Adopt an attitude of saying yes now and figuring out the details later. Then you'll start to feel more satisfied with life.

Your passion can be that you want to live and experience life. Your hunger to fulfill that goal will drive you. It doesn't take a million dollars, so stay in your lane and stay focused.

Don't get distracted. Be open to what others are saying. Keep working for it, as I've been telling you all through this book.

Do what most don't do. Be true to yourself.

Fear, doubt, self-criticism, and lack of focus can be the Four Horsemen of your personal apocalypse if you let them. Anything that prevents you from reaching your ultimate goal of a Satisfied Life is the enemy. Whether these things are attacking you from within, or are coming from outside sources, remember that the antidote is to stay Passionate, Focused, and Hungry.

Be vigilant.

The more you can keep the Four Horsemen at bay, the more likely you will have a Satisfied Life.

CHAPTER SEVEN

HAVE AN ATTITUDE OF GRATITUDE

Some studies show that practicing active gratitude elevates your mental state, allowing you to be in an even higher state of receptivity and alignment with your goals.

Do you have practices like these in your day currently?

Every day you are told from a variety of sources to be grateful for what you have. Yet, so many people cannot connect to that as a value and practice in their lives.

Can you? If not, do you know what blocks you? (Do I even have to tell you to make a list?)

You can practice gratitude at any time of day. You can choose to set aside some time in the morning, mid-day, or evening. Or perhaps you might even set a few alerts on your phone as a reminder throughout the day to connect to this powerful emotion.

If you're in a high state of stress due to external circumstances, finding what there is to be grateful for in those moments can make all the difference. It can be what decides your next move. If you focus on what you perceive to be bad, the stress can catapult you into an anxiety attack and a feeling of being overwhelmed. Or, you can access peace and perseverance by identifying what you're grateful for and expressing your gratitude out into the world.

Gratitude is a huge part of living a Satisfied Life. This includes gratitude for what you've accomplished up until now, who you intrinsically are, and what you're meant to do on this earth.

Don't resent the cards you've been dealt. Recognize the value in them, and be grateful for the opportunity to transform your pain into accomplishments. God made you exactly the way you are for a reason, and the sooner you see and acknowledge that the better off you'll be. Only you can live the life you live. Embrace those cards.

An attitude of gratitude can get you ahead in your career. It can attract your ideal partner with whom you'll grow and evolve. Feeling grateful for your body's ability to move and function can help you lose the weight you've been trying to get off for years. Your body hears you, so if you think or speak negatively of it, trust me, it knows.

It's not the honors, prizes, or the fancy outer trappings of life that ultimately nourish your being. It's having the *gratitude* of knowing that you can be trusted, that you never have to fear the truth, and that the bedrock of your very being is good.

Be careful not to use gratitude as a way to avoid your feelings just because you think it sounds better to say you're grateful instead of feeling sad, angry, or disappointed. The cool thing here is that our negative emotions and gratitude can coexist.

You can be a child, upset about some misfortune while simultaneously grateful for the roof over your head and the food on the table.

But don't jump prematurely to saying you're grateful for an unfortunate occurrence (like a breakup, for example) without also acknowledging the sadness you're feeling. Yes, eventually, gratitude will come, and it will all make sense, but if you're feeling down, know that is okay. Acknowledge those feelings.

Tomorrow is another day, and you can always find the good in any situation.

Resilience is born from perspective.

Your decision here will either work in your favor or fight against you over and over again, just as it is for all of these practices shared in this book.

You are a gift to this world. Be grateful for that gift.

CHAPTER EIGHT

ARE YOU FEELING LUCKY, PUNK?

Have you ever witnessed someone attribute another's success as luck? Have you ever done it yourself?

Sometimes people see someone who's living a life they desire and are quick to identify them as lucky. It's easier to attribute that success to luck instead of taking ownership of their lack of passion, focus, and hunger.

"Working harder and smarter than others is usually what makes people lucky."

There are three ways to find the luck that will lead to your ultimate success:

First, work harder and smarter than others.

Second, work harder and smarter than others.

Third, work harder and smarter than others.

Lucky people show up and work while others sleep. They also sleep when they know they need it and optimize performance. Don't get so caught up in work that you forget to prioritize your wellness along the way. No one would categorize someone who's experienced a heart attack from overworking as "lucky." Fairytales have perpetuated the concept of luck. Take Cinderella, for example. She shows up at the ball, and the prince falls in love with her. Lucky, right? Not so much. Don't disregard all the years of work she put in for her stepmother up until that ball. She made herself into the kind of person a prince would fall in love with.

Even one-hit wonders have put in years of work before their songs hit number one. "Overnight success" stories almost always come with a backstory of an enormous amount of work.

Many people who use the label "lucky" just don't want to put in the work themselves. It's like blaming a lack of time instead of prioritizing key tasks when you attribute success and satisfaction to luck instead of work ethic.

There is something to be said for being in the right place at the right time. There is an element of "luck" that you can't affect. That makes it even more important that you are always prepared for that "lucky" moment. You never know when you will have that once-in-a-lifetime opportunity.

There is a well-known quote that says, says that "Luck happens when preparation meets opportunity."

Imagine you're an entrepreneur with a world-changing product. You have a prototype in the very early stages of development. You find yourself in line at a coffee shop in a conversation with someone who could take your product to the next level.

How effectively could you describe your product with just your words (and the inevitable hand gestures)?

How much more effective could you be if you actually had that prototype with you? Or photos and schematics? How much more impact would that moment have?

Like gratitude and celebrating accomplishments, expecting and preparing to be "lucky" can help you live a Satisfied Life. If you wake up with the belief you are lucky, work to be ready for that golden opportunity, you'll get ahead. And you'll be miles ahead of those who are prone to complaining and blaming life for why things don't work out.

Living a Satisfied Life will automatically trigger others into thinking you're lucky.

Why? Because your level of happiness, fulfillment, and satisfaction will be significantly higher than their own. You'll start to be able to live fully in the present moment.

Feeling lucky? Work harder and smarter, and make your luck a reality😉.

CHAPTER NINE

AND IN THE END

And in the end
The love you take
Is equal to the love you make.

~ John Lennon and Paul McCartney

What goes around, comes around. You only get out of it what you put into it. There are so many ways to say it, but it all amounts to the same thing. If you want to live a Satisfied Life, you have to put in the effort to make the necessary changes.

Everything I've shared with you in this book has led to my Satisfied Life. I strive for more while enjoying the ride because if the journey isn't enjoyable, what's the point?

Imagine setting a goal and telling yourself you can only enjoy life once you attain it -- not breathing, eating well, laughing, finding passion, loving, or anything of the like along the way.

That doesn't sound very satisfying at all. In fact, it sounds pretty miserable.

As a society, we give accolades to those who hustle their way to a heart attack. Why? The idea that if you're not busy, you are not worth as much as the next guy is a fallacy. Busy doesn't mean satisfaction. It doesn't even imply productivity either. (Remember that chapter about time?)

So you work 100 hours per week, saying it's for your kids. But if you're never home investing time with them, are you truly living a Satisfied Life? Chances are you're missing out on more than you even know. Your money won't remember you. Your family will. And they'd rather have you present to create those memories than hustling away at your job.

Life is a long journey, but don't miss out on enjoying the now. That's the good stuff.

No one ends life wishing they had spent more time at work or spent more time worrying about things they couldn't control. The biggest regret most people claim is what they didn't do – the opportunities they missed, the time they missed out on with family or pursuing love, adventure, or that one "unattainable" goal.

I asked you to work harder than other people to create your own luck. I also asked you to work *smarter*. Working harder doesn't mean put in more hours slogging away at your tasks. Invest your time wisely. Make it count.

Don't lock yourself up. Learn to express your feelings along the way. Cultivate a relationship with yourself. Examine and understand how you feel, and surround yourself with people who have the same values. This will ensure a greater happiness level.

Look happiness in the face and know it's a choice. Enjoy the journey to your goal. Remember, you get to decide how to spend every day. You choose how to invest each moment of that day.

Smile. Right now. Don't think about it. Just do it.

There, you affected the chemicals in your brain -- even if just a little bit -- you put more joy in this moment than the one before it.

Don't stay stuck in old patterns and mindsets that inhibit your level of happiness.

Open yourself to change and let happiness in.

You may not have control of everything around you, but you have complete control of your actions and reactions.

You choose, with each moment, to grow or to stay stagnant.

Make your to do list, **A TO BE LIST.....**

Every Day,

Embrace These Values,

and You Will Achieve Your

Most Satisfied Life...

THANK YOU FOR READING MY BOOK!

DOWNLOAD YOUR FREE GIFTS

Read This First

Just to say thanks for buying and reading my book, I would like to give you a few free bonus gifts, no strings attached!

To Download Now, Visit:

www.GetYourSatisfactionBook.com/Freegift

I appreciate your interest in my book, and I value your feedback as it helps me improve future versions of this book. I would appreciate it if you could leave your invaluable review on Amazon.com with your feedback. Thank you!

www.ingramcontent.com/pod-product-compliance
Lightning Source LLC
LaVergne TN
LVHW051017080826
845145LV00009B/2671

* 9 7 8 1 7 3 6 5 4 9 1 2 4 *